AF574409

ENOUGH SAID

1980 PHOTOGRAPH BY TOM GIRARDOT

Philip Whalen
ENOUGH SAID

FLUCTUAT NEC MERGITUR

Poems 1974–1979

Grey Fox Press
San Francisco • 1980

LIBRARY OF CONGRESS
CATALOGING IN PUBLICATION DATA:

Whalen, Philip.
Enough said.

I. Title.
PS3545.H117E56 811'.54
ISBN 0-912516-48-8 (lim. ed.)
ISBN 0-912516-49-6 (pbk.)

The publication of this book was partially supported by a grant from the National Endowment for the Arts, Washington, D.C., a federal agency.

to

Joanne Elizabeth Kyger

Contents

Preface

The most interesting thing about this book is that it was written under ideal conditions. The author was living a life of elegant retirement in the character of a Zen Buddhist priest at the Hossen Temple in San Francisco and at the monastery of Zenshinji at Tassajara Springs, far in the mountains east of the Big Sur. Given ideal conditions, how could life be anything but a joyous round of pleasure. What could possibly go wrong.

At the top of the hill above the Third Culvert (counting from the first one over Cabarga Creek as one ascends the road to and from Tassajara) I sat down for a minute to consider what's possible. A sentence, a word, a monkey flower. Sun heats; wind cools, simultaneously. What am I after. From this point the road is uphill and downhill. The flowers are too pale to be monkey flowers. They aren't the exact color of wild azaleas. My ears fry in the sunlight. There are monkey flowers no matter what I say, just as K. M. still has a terrible cough this morning. Wild larkspurs have three different shades of blue.

Early the next morning I find that my brains have come loose and are floating up against the skull bones, gently bumping and knocking with the motions of the tide. I used to believe that I could do anything so long as I really understood that there'd be consequences, whether pleasant or unpleasant, consequences of specific size, shape, color and duration. They were to be accepted and digested. (People used to say, "Never buy anything you can't eat.") Now I'm uncertain whether all the consequences of any—even the simplest—action can be known immediately; I fear that some of the smaller details which one may have overlooked may bring about a disaster which will arrive at the door on some innocently beautiful Sunday morning. Why not.

At the turnout above the Third Culvert I found a set of *juzu* beads which I hadn't realized leaving or losing. There they were drying in the sun beside variegated lupine flowers. At sundown that day I noted that a great wind was blowing lumps and sheets of cloud across the narrow sky; maybe that's all that was scheduled to happen that day. Later the air was fresh and still. The full moon appeared.

Returned to the city after many months I find too many things in my rooms and not enough air. What can be is a slice of Nob Hill in the distance. Radio delivers KJAZ without hesitation. No ideas or anything; imported beer. There was a visit to the rhododendrons blooming in the Park. In Stockton Street, Gregory Corso hollers to me from the window of his mother-in-law's blue station wagon, also blooming. (Max doesn't say hello but appears and disappears, grinning, from under an Army blanket on the floor of the car behind his father's seat.) Ideal conditions prevail in the city and in the country. I continue, after all; and the consequences.

PW
Tassajara / San Francisco
1980

ENOUGH SAID
Poems 1974–1979

Murals Not Yet Dreamed

The First Panel is occupied with Storm and Night Battle:
Handsome Allegorical Embellishments fruits and flowers
Antique masks and fantastic animals or birds amid trailing
vines and scallop shells, leaves, Wild Men, Trophies,
Instruments of Music profusely beribboned and garlanded
The whole supported on sculptured brackets or consoles
Decorated with partially draped Atlantids wreathed with
oaken crowns

The Second Panel shews the arrival of the King
And the fit is on him
He shouts for the Countess of Suffolk who lies ill in her room
Lord Townshend, Sir Robert Walpole and the Duke of
Newcastle
Approach from the right, bearing a petition
Sir Robert stares into the clear blue eyes of Queen Caroline
Dressed in seventy or eighty yards of handmade Flemish lace and
Silk brocade, a young fortune in pearls and diamonds and a couple
Of egret feathers. Lord Hervey as Vice Chamberlain preens
And simpers at her side all blue velvet and lavender silk

The Third Panel crashes down in splinters and torn canvas
I open fire with my Sten gun, screeching defiance
As they mow me down.

11-12:VI:74

How To Be Successful & Happy Without Anybody Else Finding out About It

I was falling asleep in my chair
Now I lie on the floor, ruminating ideas of life's brevity
The feeble intensity of enormous ambition
Hasleton Brasler said he'd be over
He had to pick up his car and take a haircut
You understand what I'm talking about . . .
"including the power tools"
There's no excuse for an imitation of Billie Holiday.

Think of grass, a half acre of weeds, lawn, eucalyptus trees
Pink lilies on leafless thick red stems, all in a row
Appearing "spontaneously" (not from a regular bed or trench
Of specially cultivated earth. You remember what I'm talking
About, you've been there, but maybe not in lily season)

A freezing cold morning, throat and sinuses "burning"
Hasleton Brasler was uncertain: Thursday or Saturday.
He didn't want tea or whiskey. He had forgotten why he
wanted to see me.

My sleep wrecked with difficult dreams,
Managing crowds of friends, trying to organize them
Interrupted (wakened) by scene with (who?) again
Persuade, explain, hopeless
The lilies shove right up out of the grass
Where one expects flat ground, these big
Vegetable telephone rockets, their irregular line
Fat rutabaga bulbs clearing the surface of the ground
Swelling and subdividing

Probably listening to Hasleton Brasler last night
Trying to come up with helpful suggestions for "coping" with
his difficulties.

With so little rain the lilies will be late this year.
Why don't I go home to Oregon?
Seventy or eighty feet of "naked ladies" all in a row: Amaryllis

"... brought the apples you wanted ...
... more tomorrow," Theocritus says.

6:IX:74

Organized Crime

I looked inside the refrigerator and said, "Credit Lyonnais,"
And shut the insulated door (ga-lunk).
Characters in somebody's novels, people who amounted
To anything at all have big accounts in the Banque de
L'Indo-Chine

Let's all try to do better!
All my incandescent armor
From invidious glebe ration confusion
Minshew, Peabody, reach and fine
Inviolably now.

As the Duchess told the magazine,
"One can never be too thin nor too rich."

October-November 1974

Compulsive Obligatory Paranoia Flashes

While ever at my back I hear Time's winged chariot,
More or less skilfully guided by Henry and Claire Booth Luce
He (Agni, the Hindu god of fire) said,
"Why have ye (Devas) brought me to birth?"
They answered, "To keep watch."

Tomatoes must be gently wrapped in suitable coverings
And shut up in a dark place like mad men
Where they ripen

The world is a willful Idea? I'm after something;
Bright changing shadow
(Everything to eat except desire)

> "The last time I saw him his face and head
> Were completely depilated and all his features gross
> And swollen like Gene Sibelius."
> "*Jean,*" somebody said. "Or *Jan*?"
> "What are you, some kind of intellectual?"

September-December 1974

Ice Plant

A freezing factory; somebody else's jewels
Used in an attempt to incriminate

Fat shaving brush flower

7:XI:74

Conclusions

1

". . . and what did they do?
cut the face right off
the front of his head . . ."

2

When the sun and the moon
Fall from her hands
Where shall we run

25:V:75

For Clark Coolidge

tick
notch
fanrandole
A Venetian lantern rhyme
Perfume wild thyme gland of youth
Clara Wilkes Booth, Founderess
Red Cross and Salvation Army
Clara Barton Batten Durstine & Osborn
incunabula tightrope novel of blank mind
born clear and smooth   not a wedge in sight
whelms. qualms. nick.
(scotch)

sham

5:VI:75

A Crackling

Taken by twos who wrote it all
Frying and twisting finally curly animal crystal
Some kind of grease ghost
Perfectly organized vehicle for squares of salt
And a beer with a secret number of drops of vinegar
    in which red chili peppers lie embalmed
Religiously shaken (aspergill)
Cut-glass cruet from the caster set

or 220 volts direct current
(the Outraged Majesty of the Law
and Public Opinion)
fries brains and all or pellets of cyanide crystals
the size of pigeon eggs drop into acid bath
Medea's fountain of youth
(Boiled King.)

5:VI:75

Brutal Landscape

O drown minus
        (this doesn't make any sense except in Harlan County
        or a classical dictionary. . . Rhadamanthis/Aides)
Drown bull-headed S.O.B. &c.
Drown Midas
        the Bakeoven Road!
        hot clay walls
        leafless dry weed chasm
        (doesn't make any sense except in Wasco County)
Shaniko to Maupin, there's no creek on the map
Nothing but yellow-orange dirt: very small mountains of
    nowhere
Because of The Pioneers and the trout in Tygh Creek
Beanie and Millard at Wapinitia
And Mrs B in her white satin gown
Leading the Mysteries of the Great White Shrine
        (That road actually a short-cut to Madras
        Where she sold McCormick-Deering combines)
Make a loop from Arlington back to The Dalles
Without going through Madras at all, where *die Aegyptische*
    Helen . . .

But now sirens under my window stop at nothing
A burning automobile right here in Lily Alley: *Erlkönig*
        (". . . a woman's body, high concentration of drugs,
        alchohol and radioactive substances . . ." in some other
        state, the radio continues, "unexpected
        outbreak of respiratory arrests")
        "Take, O take them lips AWAY"
        Sunyata, all voided out eyes of Little Orphan Annie

Certain things make a great deal of sense in Topeka. Or else.

7:VIII:75-24:I:77

Dorje Quandary

When I can't breathe it means the north wind is blowing
When I can't sleep the full moon shines.
While trying to sleep forget what I was trying to remember:
Dreamy search for what isn't lost if it's forgotten
Why it can't be found.

Twenty years from now, should I say the same
(Seven-try-one)
Set five-point vajra in direct sun
Orient north and south: results instantaneously
As it is, it is you.

22:VIII:75

The Radio Again

It wasn't in the cards
That today should go the way I want
Not in the cards.
I can't complain about the way it went.

"It says right on the box"
as her voice tells us her name is Ethel

Lady, it is what the lawyers call a self-serving document

"Oh yes, I always buy this kind."

Voice, tell us
The name of the earth.

November 1975-January 1976

Somebody Else's Problem Bothers Me

Warm sun and chilly air, water is low and the creek is clear
Will I accidentally drop a jade ring in the creek
All the new stones glaring light and airplanes
Shall I drop my gold crown in the pool?
Have I derailed my train of thought?
A rock with an elephant's forehead!
Silver turquoise ring dropped into monk's kimono sleeve
What can we answer?

Yellow tin chimneys.

White-crowned sparrows.

Everything a-tilt.

26:III:76

Bead

Aimless
Wet finger no foresight
Small craft warning from Telephone Company
Earth
Bear
        Birth
          O
        Breath
          and
        Bread
(Careless wet finger again)

28:III:76

La Jolla in the Morning

For Bill Berkson

A mockingbird a swimming pool a tennis court
A minute putting-green an ocean among subtropical flowers
The last of California built for Ginger Rogers
The nineteen-thirties completely restored
Subliminal throb of pool filter pump
Gentle roar of heavy traffic among hibiscus bulldozer

Beige/pink telephone lives with other furniture beside the pool
Lost fountain pen lies on silk upholstered chair that is
Fond of rich tea cakes and chocolate creams
A chair that might live in remotest Connecticut
Limp money death in beautiful clothes
Remote from The Dalles or La Jolla

Top of the yacht's mast connects with sharp
Trolley wire/sea/sky line
The outside of the window frame
Inexplicably adorned with brown wood Della Robbia wreath
Glass reflects a yacht not yet in sight
I must lean forward to see the first one
Making for Scripps Oceanographical Institute
Where it'll be wrapped in plastic foam
Then loaded onto the Boston plane with its owner
A regatta this weekend in New London

Imagine how to be free of the thought which is to say
Free from the past free from hankering after some future
Bait (or hooked for a second) actually seeing
Elaborated floral rococo handles on an ordinary
Wooden chest of drawers

which become Alex Katz:

Three scallops of green bushes
Flat against the ocean's flat horizon
And happily not exactly joining the same line reflected
In the imperfect window glass wavy and uneven so the boat's
image
And that compulsively vacant (I mean tyrannical) sky/sea
Nonexistent boundary (tyrannical to our eyes,
Which have been taught to see)
Becomes its imaginary self and we are saved again. Whew!

The benefits of travel are immediate; a battleship or
Minesweeper on the horizon among mockingbirds
(*Liebestraum*
Or Liederkrantz?) twisted around the window frame
Aimless luxury, swollen details ultimately blank
Cement *putti* not only cold but hollow
To deceive the eye, which pretends to be delighted
For maybe thirty seconds

Here is the world before the war, quite different from
San Francisco
Where we have another style, young rich and careless
Robbery and murder right out in the street
A city hall where a cardinal-archbishop ought to live
A Custom House and a Federal Court that might house Borgias
Or a pope in armor on horseback.

April 1976-January 1977

Powell & Market

Fat man waves tiny Bible
Shouting threats about Jesus.
Nearby, a younger, thinner man (high on something else?)
Starts undressing.

20:XII:76

Defective Circles

Electric clock died in the night
Big low-pressure system high winds and rain barge through
Present world, wake up in the dark 12:05
". . . made by a magic no handmakers know. . ."
Shall I remember that when I get back from the bathroom?
Lines of groovy poem around me
Did I know who I was where then?
12:05 daylight, don't care much about who I am
What I'm supposed to be doing
Still humming and warm to the touch
Neither of us making any sense.

12:III:77

Many Pages Must Be Thrown Away

To talk about the green roof
Next to the silvery blue house—pointless
Because the way the light hits them
There are more colors anyhow—
Porpoise flank, eye of albacore

Air all new and clean
Sharp edges of Berkeley reappear
Among bridge cable web and thrum
Sundown crosslight bird clank
City Hall dome throbs and bulges
Opera House whale eyes look west
Suave white geometry lid of cathedral
Translucent, incandescent

I ascend to the roof to look again
Light as it is at Tangiers, they say,
Straight across the town
Flat up against walls doors hills

Against which waves flash explode eastward
Ocean rushing towards Donner Pass

14-23:IV:77

Obsolete Models

Now the hours of my life grow small
Shoddy months and threadbare years
A favorite pet universe that ought to be "put to sleep"
By the vet; gracefully relinquished.

I say, "Something eludes me
Something is right over there–someplace."
A drop of mercury slides very smoothly away
A description slightly out of focus

At least there are nasturtiums again
Disc leaves dusty green
More entertaining than many another
Verdigris

What do I want
What am I really after
Sometimes a tree answers.

18-19:IV:77
San Francisco

The Congress of Vienna

What's happening continues
"All still going on out there"
Last night eclipsed the moon
In order to say "Earth is a celestial disc
Over–not under–the moon"

Let's reconvene the Congress of Vienna
Nasturtiums at Schoenbrunn
Posies for Prince Metternich
Nosegays for Prince Talleyrand

On the floor a platter of chicken,
Thin elegant gravy, all of us eating
Most of us resigned to having a third helping
Long-haired grey cat walks into the dish, lies down
Rolls about in the sauce
Universal horror and chagrin!
We try to clean it with a big bath towel
If it licks up too much gravy the cat will have the gout
Annoyance, mirth, and worry

As long as I do not look out the window,
Great things, weird sounds,
High deeds in Lily Alley:
"You there track book!
Brat work! Dropsy!
Dim attending brunt or charred bird."
"What did you have for dinner?"
"Chard quiche."
"Hey there! 1878!"
"Eighteen seventy ate three, hey? There."
Quick change cymbal
". . . the difference to me!"

What though my eyes are blind with age and simple-
mindedness?
Death's crumby fingers insinuating fate
Tumescent sentences to say, to want to say,
"Flower: The world here becomes pond lilies
Tall yellow iris and trade for a world of rhododendrons
Total experience of wealth beyond rich and poor
Monterey cypress and black pine cliffs
Birdshadows trill and marble hallelujah
Out beyond the throne of time.

San Francisco
4:IV-11:V:77

Lines for a Celebrated Poet

I go into the closet and shut the door.
I put on mother's clothes; then I can hear her,
Talking to me plain as ever.

My liver trembles on a golden tray
Before the Chief Justice of The United States
My kidneys float in a candy jar with an ornamental top,
Lewis County Fairgrounds, Chehalis, Washington;
Brains under several pounds of mercury in a crock
"What the fairies talk and murmur
That we understand though mumbled. . ."

Never in Leadville
Never in Lubbock
Never in Twentynine Palms

27-28:V:77

"Past Ruin'd Ilion"

Past ancient dusty Antigua bright blue water above Port Royal
Beyond Terre Haute the legendary city
Abandoned to the winds of moon by Tom Field and Cubby
  Selby
Olson said that Cubby Selby walked up the road all alone
Wearing a baseball glove, tossing a ball in the air
As he approached the campus of Black Mountain College
Left his luggage at the station to await developments
If it wasn't Cubby Selby it was that guy
Who later wrote his recollections of Franz Kline
So much for reminiscences of the great
  "Tossing a ball in the air and catching it. Beautiful."

It probably was Fielding Dawson
Anyway, somebody burned down Pass Christian, Mississippi
Probably not Hubert Selby, Jr
Past the barriers of time and the ruining of Denver
The demolition of Portland (Oregon)
The voice of Nellie Melba echoing in the Parthenon
Sara Bernhardt at the Erechtheum Judy Garland
At the Orpheum
Viciously entangled; everything deliberately scrambled
There is complete exact beauty and satisfaction
Even the empty shells are beautiful to contemplate,

(DESUNT CETERA)

Port Townsend
11-12 July 1977

Garden Cottage #1

Chill morning moonlight garden by Douanier Rousseau
Some weird bird or animal cries at 3 A.M.
Lost, meaningless, wild.
Temporarily the moon-window in the sleeping loft
Composes a picture of mountains and tree tops
In the Chinese taste, although an edge of the roof cuts a chord
Out of the circle.
If I should die the picture would decompose
The window just be a hole in a wall
The mountains would be someplace else
This probably is all about a poem I wrote sixteen years ago.

Tassajara
September-October 1977

"Back to Normalcy"

My ear stretches out across limitless space and time
To meet the fly's feet coming to walk on it
The cat opens an eye and shuts it
That much meaning, use or significance

Wind chime, hawk's cry
Pounding metal generator
Bell and board rehearsing bluejays
Dana, phoning, shouts "You mean fiberglass?"
Telephone grapeleaves shake together
Dull blond sycamore sunshine
Dana says, "All you guys bliss out
Behind the carrot and raisin salad?"
Brown dumb leaves fall on bright ferns
New and thick since the fire.

Tassajara
8-11:XI:77

"I Used to Work in Chicago"

In a private collection
Hans Memling or Dierck Bouts:
"Madonna & Child, with Sonny Rollins"
A gloss on the Buddhist Hybrid Sanskrit
Anutpattikadharmksanti
"acquiescence in the principle
That the *dharmas* do not come into being"
(Unless of course there's an acceleration of energy)
Until vast black basalt griffin bull with face of
Beard crown of man steps forward

San Francisco
22:XII:77

Tears and Recriminations

How charming the sticky sweat
The overheated stove the deranged sensibilities
The lady student suspended from College as
"Morally insensate"
As two lovely oranges in a little basket lined with a folded
Red linen napkin

". . . but only if it gratifies your inmost wish," I said
And the saltine being smeared with peanut butter
Broke in two

Tassajara
5:II:78

Waste. Profligacy. Fatuity.

We get ourselves into a mess when we say
"Thank God that's over," "Never again will I do thus & so."
Nothing is over or under; things is and then change,
We think of ourselves as we used to be
What is we now?
Bright cold moon
Too much dinner
Unlimited cookies
Baked bananas
Booby Pie
Cinnamon infested coffee (blarp)
And a salad full of nasty little surprises
  (Creepy croutons, dead beans,
  Unidentified glips, clots, paps)

("To think that anyone could SAY such a thing, much less write it down!")

19-20:II:78
Tassajara

Discriminations

Earliest morning hot moonlight
A catastrophe, the garden too theatrical
Feels wild, unearthly
H. P. Lovecraft could use his favorite adjective:
"Eldritch"

The "shooting-star" flowers that Mama used to call "bird-bills"
Bloom around the Hogback graveyard
Suzuki Roshi's great seamless monument
Wild cyclamen, actually, as in the *Palatine Anthology*
I go home to mend my *rakusu* with golden thread.

Tassajara
24:II:78

Wandering Outside

Purple flags for the luxurious color
Extravagant form; and then I calmly
Empty dead tea leaves into the toilet
I hate the world I hate myself the dragon wind
I allow everything to happen

I want luxury, extravagance, to use
To give to you,
A wild naked leap in moonlight surf
Wildflower meadow, swim in alpine lake
Stand under waterfall

André Gide I always think of as dried salmon
Stringy and smoky, but there he is:

> "going up the bed of a mountain torrent
> to a waterfall under which I rushed
> as soon as I could undress. The icy water,
> falling from a height,
> stung like hail . . ."

In the character of Mongaku Shonin—
High passion, murder, and political intrigue

Tassajara
17:III:78

Homage to St. Patrick, García Lorca, & the Itinerant Grocer

For M-D. Schneider

A big part of this page (a big part of my head)
Is missing. That cabin where I expected to sit in the
Woods and write a novel got sold
            out from under my imagination

I had it all figured out
            in the green filter of a vine-maple shade
The itinerant grocer would arrive every week
There was no doubt in my mind that I'd have money
To trade for cabbages and bread

Where did that vision take place—maybe Arizona
            Or New Mexico, where trees are much appreciated—

I looked forward to having many of my own
Possessed them in a nonexistent future green world of lovely
   prose
Lost them in actual present poems in Berkeley
All changed, all strange, all new; none green.

Tassajara
17:III:78

What About It?

When I began to grow old I searched out the Land
Of the Gods in the West, where our people have always said
it is.
Once I floated there on the water. Once I flew there.
I heard their music and saw the magic dancing.
They appeared in many shapes; once as *kachina,*
Once I could only see shining feet and radiant clothes
Their houses blend into water, trees and stone.
A curtain moved. Water fell in certain order.
Sometimes there was a great mirror of polished bronze.
Other messages were smell of *hinoki, sugi,* gingko
Newly watered stones.
The land itself delivers a certain intelligence.

How embarrassing to note that four days are gone.
All I can say right now is I can see clouds in the sky
If I stand still and look out the window.
Diane Di Prima came and told me, "If we leave
Two hours of the day open for them
The poems will come in or out or however;
Anyway, to devote time in return for a place
That makes us accessible to them."

San Francisco
17-28:IV:78

The Laundry Area

Each time I hang up a washboard
The slenderest thread of cold water
Runs down my wrist and into my armpit
Without wetting my clothes.

Tassajara
22:III:78

Cynical Song

You do what you do
Fucky-ducky
You do it anyhow
People don't like it
Fucky-ducky
People like it
Fucky-ducky
You do what you do
Fucky-ducky

San Francisco
29:IV:78

"Can't You Be a Little More Selective?"

When you break it
Make sure it comes apart
Stop at nothing

Is there something there a broken egg

"Adipose muchachos
Compañeros de ma vida,"

Three months and nearly a fourth are spent
Or lost or otherwise missing
They had no more than a conventional existence?
Fluctuat nec mergitur?
And then
The little boat emerges from the Tunnel of Love
All blush and giggle and sweaty
Into the brilliant day.

San Francisco
3-4:VI:78

insist there be a voice, then listen

*

X: "You can do everything."
Y: "I'm so glad. One day,
I shall buy a full gallon of Best Foods Mayonnaise."

*

Budweiser: used egg
New bicycle. Proudly.
Who.

*

X: Wouldn't it be strange
Never to go back to that building
Revisit (for example) New Mexico
Or Kyoto every year, commencing now.
Y: Whatever for? & why "strange"?
There's no reason to go back—you didn't
Leave your hat, or lose your watch?
X: Monstrous. Gross. Un-natural.
Love comes back to dote and sigh,
"If only . . ."

*

The orphan scottie didn't quite follow me out the door—whether he's getting used to the idea that he shouldn't run out into the street . . . was he discouraged by the sight of that steep brick stairway or was he resigned to the idea that I (like his recent master) was abandoning him—who knows? I worry about that dog, unable to care sincerely about little else beyond the pleasure of writing it here.

The dog is helpless, fat, and lost; seemingly aware that he's temporarily safe and generally admired, but not particularly loved? no specific (as once two) person(s) he must love in return;

*

X: Where has caring gone.
Y: Back to Montana, in a Volkswagen bug.

*

I love you very much
But sometimes I love you even more from a distance
Never to the vanishing point

*

It's true, as Duncan used to say,
We need permission for what we do
Next we must grab permission by the horns & hang on
It isn't just a grant, a gift, a boon, grab it and run
Before they change their minds
PARCAE
MOIRA
Hang on while he goes through all
His demonic changes,
Old what's his name, out of the sea
Will be obliged to say what's true
If you can keep hold and listen.
You see only flashing in the air from the jewels
That I'm wearing a bear triangle upside down
Gold and silver sleep; diamonds wake.
I see you in spite of my wrinkled eyes

*

Now the little dog is attached by his leash to the leg of a yellow upholstered wing-chair in the Flop Room. He lies on the floor, most of the time, dejected—and sensible of a general (if gentle) rejection. Some dog enthusiasts cart him out for a walk but they bring him back too soon and set him in the corner again like a fern. There he must await developments. He has clean water in a yellow plastic dish. The dish is probably clean enough for a dog but it looks dingy and sad. The dog's various wounds, received in a recent fight, have been treated several times by a vet and are healing.

There is food and care and endlessly interrupted and scattered attention. The little dog seems indifferent—dopey and sad. Lucy says she's doing her best to find a home for him. Why does his appearance trouble me. He's only a dog, and everything that can be done for him is being done.

10:VI-8:VIII:78

The Inspection of the Mind in June

All of me that there is makes a shadow.

San Francisco
14:VI:78

Treading More Water

It is very hard to understand that
We are where we are at; I am here intentionally
Can you want to do anything
What were you doing. Standing around talking
Greater downtown Chehalis
Night or late-blooming seriously
Let us fall back and regroup (Laocoön)

The mad King of Ireland
Suibhne could fly
That is flying was a symptom of his madness
He lived in a tree; he ate nothing at all.
Crowned.

Start again. Direct the imagination
A knotted mass of grey yarn and very delicate blood vessels
Forward (there's no other direction)
Enclosed please find the pig
"fantastically dressed up with flowers"
"mad, crowned with weeds and flowers"
"mad, bedecked with weeds"
"mad, (fantastically dressed with weeds)"

Seven minutes from now. You hear the words.
"Caught between Sybil and Charisma"
I am grown invisible and very wise

San Francisco
11:VII:78

I Can Look Any Way I Feel Like

Unless you have one lifetime friend
Whose business is the production of "lewd shows," for example
A friend you associate with your childhood in a provincial town
A place much different in color and style from what you are seeing now
It would be hard to guess what kind of creature you might be.
If you are very rich you own the building (or the ground under it)
Where the show takes place; if you are very poor, maybe you're
Working for your friend or have declined a job with his troupe

He knows you and knew your folks and you knew his
And sometimes you remember you owe him or he owes you ten dollars

His picture appears on the front page once a decade:

PORN KING ARRAIGNED
or
CONGRESSMAN WINS HEAVY IN WHATCOM COUNTY

People tease you for a few days about "Your friend,
The smut pedlar"
"Your pal, Senator X." They are the friends that you have now.

28:VII:78

The Holding Pattern

Invidious joys all sealed in veins
On top of the mailbox Herman Street; what's more,
Two of the big orchid plants bloom all through May
And this far into June.
One is mostly white with pinky-lavender edge to its lip
Other is off-orange yellow with tawny markings
Later, M. tells me that she gave them to Suzuki Roshi,
"Years ago—cymbidium: They need seven years to grow
Before they'll bloom."

12:VI, 23:VIII:78

What? Writing in the Dining Room?

One long table supported by three sets of winged lions;
Each lion has a single, enormous clawed foot
Their faces resemble those of American highschool students
Expressing rage, horror, disbelief
Here might be kings and commisars affixing signatures and
  seals
To important documents of state.

I imagine a dream recollection of my father
Telling his mother-in-law a plan of collecting 50¢ per night
From every guest in his house.
Hot northwind flaps my clothes.

Is there a way whereby I can stop stoning myself
Get on with my work? I want to write this
I refuse to do anything else as long as I want to
Write this it is important and horrible and meaningless . . . .

There.
"DON'T MOVE"
i.e. by not moving I lend some shade
make a lap for the baby or for the cat
My shoes are set in a row, not going anywhere
As if I'd gone without them
Carted directly to hospital or morgue
To little magic nonexistent worlds
Pagan Rome
Nothing reappeared; two is lost
"The time has come and went," she said
Unable to keep our engagement for lunch

The little dog has gone to live in Visalia.
Everybody misses him, of course.

15-24:IX:78

How Many Is Real

Whether we intended it or liked it or wanted it
We are part of a circle that stands beyond life and death
Happening whether we will or no
We can't break it, we are seldom aware of it
And it looks clearest to people beyond its edge.
They are included in it
Whether or not they know

11:X:78

Rodomontade

Did you sleep. Did the same person
wake
"I CAN HEAR SOMEBODY BREATHING."
The day swells and contracts tidally
With the sun.

While not able to go ahead I divide
Spread out from ears east and west parallel
To the wall, sometimes far above and beyond it
I don't care about time, either

Each page of the book splits along the edge
To reveal many thin sheets inside:
Color reproductions, drawings, more and newer messages
Brighter words

San Francisco
15:XI:78

Lost Fragments from *The Impatient Monument*

"They're all out there on this island, see, and they're high, see . . ."

*

"You mean if I went down to that Opera House
And spent a lot of money
The Sugarplum Fairy would do her dance for me?
You must imagine that I'm quite naive . . ."

*

A species of pumpkin or a yellow melon?
Gourd? Cucurbit?
Anise flowers, their suspended
Bursts of yellow plinks . . .

*

Loud buds in bird tree
Unreliable deities flung
One specific light-point
Beside the turret roof
The morning star

*

In the picture
The road is a tree
Branching and leaving.

San Francisco
August-November 1978

What's New?

We keep forgetting the world is alive
Being the same as we
The coathanger and kimono leap off the rail
Hurl themselves to the floor

Instead of the usual instant anger
I pause to admire this prodigy of nature
The kimono flowing in strange billows and festoons
Falling timelessly (if I say so) to the closet floor.

A couple weeks later I'm flailing about
The rug rippled and ruched, table cockeyed
Something tips over, I (furious) grab, rush,
Breathless dark living room
Why can't you, what's to stop your doing
Whatever you want to do—collect SOMETHING
Fill in the blanks later, unexpected brilliant excursions
And back again to the central trunk or channel

Watching the "waterfall" (more accurately, "water curtain")
In Beale St. PGE has done something to my head
I see myself, all persons, animals, trees &c
FALLING through space, dividing and disintegrating
Halfway down, some are shattered on the first step of the
  "fall"
Fragments thrown into the narrow pool next below
  "inevitably"
And then pumped, I suppose, to some tank or pool (roof
  garden?)
Above.

I like to think there's a garden and pond,
Plain green shrubs, maybe azaleas or camellias in tubs
Doors from the company restaurant open onto it
The pond a formal baroque design as at Inoda Coffee Shop
  in Kyoto
White smooth concrete framing it, mechanical but pleasing
("Grooming displacement behavior"?)

After murdering Kesa Gozen—by his own mistake
But her design—Endo Morito stood under the waterfall
Three weeks in a row, invoking Fudo Myo-o
And came out as Mongaku Shonin the famous monk
Who went really crazy with political intrigue
Lost everything at last and died in exile,
Sado Island, 1193.

4,27:XII:78

makes Friedrich Schiller, his personal
Oeconomy almost overrun by tubercle baccilli
Proclaim joy out of Elysium
Joy and brotherhood also drive Schopenhauer,
And Nietzsche, to suicide
Sparks Wagner's megalomaniac theatricals
With humanity as "given"
Expect nothing but trouble: No omelet from rotten eggs
4:31 A.M. war, murder, misery,
But somebody recently arranged eggs without cholesterol
("O King, live forever!")
To take care of your plugged-up veins
Gibbon says, ". . . the wisdom and authority of the
Legislator are seldom victorious in a contest
With the vigilant dexterity of private interest."

San Francisco
6:I:79

Welcome Back to the Monastery

A wildly crowded noisy breakfast
Sixty people sounding like 7500 in the highschool gymnasium
A small town in Arkansas where the people haven't seen each other
In a long time

"Just lucky enough to have thought about bringing this little bit of lunch with us—few scraps of fried chicken, 3 or 4 pounds of potato salad, salami sandwiches, potato chips, dill pickles and some chocolate chip cookies, in case the dinner was late or they wasn't anything planned. . ."

I wished for nasturtium seeds
They appear spontaneously *via* interoffice mail
Neurotic smoke alarm gibbers in the zendo
Its batteries going stale
Every morning cold air on my shaved head
Wakes me before the alarm clock
Can you hear the echo? Do you see the reflection?

Tassajara
13-15:I:79

Violins in Chaos?

Yes, now I go ahead,
Words appear and all a living world beside:
Not exactly a peak-out but a distinct blip
On an otherwise flat curve
Knobby leaf mud curtain grows on steep rock
Then lichens, moss, ferns, in Darwinian succession
A tough wide-leaved succulent lays down on top
To hide the details

OLDE SONG: "I went & { closed the window / pulled the curtain / put out the light }

So he shouldn't see my Fancy"

I didn't remember to say, that
The most brilliant white light sounds
Like the shattering of a huge pane of glass
Water makes neat crystal helmet over the rock

Tassajara
20-22:I:79

Litany of the Candy Infant of Geneva

Sweet jewel baby
Darling candy crown
Sticky luscious orb
Sparkly scepter
Golden bib of holiness pray for us
Chocolate baby pray for us
Tears of KARO pray for us
Crème Yvette wee-wee pray for us
Fondant fundament pray for us
Rum slobber pray for us
Snot of slivovitz pray for us
White crème de menthe sweat pray for us
Yummy baby pray for us
Gown of marzipan shelter us
While we suck you forever!

Tassajara
27:I:79

Homage to Sosa-No-Wo-No-Omikoto

My left thumb is cut and sore today so that
I found myself peeling an orange with my right hand
West to east around the globe
Seeing that great Kami-samma "flaying a piebald
Colt of heaven with the backward flaying,"
Just as the *Nihongi* says.

31:I:79

The Bay Trees Were About To Bloom

For each of us there is a place
Wherein we will tolerate no disorder.
We habitually clean and reorder it,
But we allow many other surfaces and regions
To grow dusty, rank and wild.

So I walk as far as a clump of bay trees
Beside the creek's milky sunshine
To hunt for words under the stones
Blessing the demons also that they may be freed
From Hell and demonic being
As I might be a cop, "Awright, move it along, folks,
It's all over, now, nothing more to see, just keep
Moving right along"

I can move along also
"Bring your little self and come on"
What I wanted to see was a section of creek
Where the west bank is a smooth basalt cliff
Huge tilted slab sticking out of the mountain
Rocks on the opposite side channel all the water
Which moves fast, not more than a foot deep,
Without sloshing or foaming.

Tassajara
11:II:79

Dying Tooth Song

Now flesh and bones burn inside my mouth
Ganges gushes from under my tongue
To fall in Siva's hair
Tooth temple of Kali
Skull dance place of Siva

Becoming Yama god of death
I become Yamantaka slayer of death
Endless wheel of waterbuckets turns
Through Babylon zodiac

I stays here turning through life and death
Offering up all this flesh and bones
Round and round

Grass greener than yellower
More birds than bluejays
Railway roar of creek
Not going to Chicago

North mountain peak
A pile of patriarchs' bones
Nyogen, Shunryu, host and guest all one heap

Tassajara
28:II:79

Rich Interior, After Thomas Mann

Why, as I was walking up the hill,
All in spring light and air
Keep seeing a glass of water standing
On a polished wooden tabletop in a big house at twilight?
As the air warms, flies and bugs hatch out
Come to sit on the top of this page, O.K.?

-2-

Yesterday's glass of water:
Standing on bare wood–surely
This was carelessly done!
There'll be a ring.
Of course, rubbing it with lemon oil will remove the mark?

This house is one cared for by "a lady who comes in" daily.
Presently it is her hand which conveys the glass
Through the next couple of handsomely furnished rooms
To the kitchen; the same hand will bring the lemon oil.
An imperfect white ring about 3/8ths of an inch wide
And almost the exact diameter of the glass
Shows where it stood. A stain.

Tassajara
3-4:III:79

Treading Water. Backing & Filling.

Here beyond the Hogback I fling myself into the creek
Water not quite chest high, cold and fast
I let the breeze dry me and all of you on this page
Written in the sun where big spiders play on the rocks
Big black butterfly with cream edged wings investigates
What is the justice of any claim? Which Real, which
"allowable"?
What I want is to get loose; not to claim or be claimed,
Falling elegantly over the rocks into the creek and gone
Silent, living, moving; sometimes roar, bubble, splash
White, clear, dark smooth, move.
I said once before, "Wet is comfort."
Probably I'm too fishy to be a seagull;
More likely a walrus or sealion.

Here is one specific contentment: shade beside a rapids
A little fall cascading down the opposite rocky bank
Fountains of the Boboli Gardens I doubt that I'll ever visit.
This leaves all Italian gardens wonderful imaginary elegance:
What the designer imagined but didn't get.

How to explain that everything is unimaginably splendid
And horrible? Or that my life at this moment is enormously
Satisfying and dreadful?
Who can resist replying, "So what else is new you got flowers
In the ass?" (O Spring, &c &c!)
& I, "Why ain't you glad I should be feeling wonderful?"
& you, exasperated, "NATURALLY you're happy—you are
heartless
And haven't a single brain in your head!"

I grow fatter and fatter and fatter, like the ox who wanted
To be a frog. He bought a tight green suit and went to sit
On a lilypad. One croak and the buttons flew off; two croaks
And the trousers burst; three croaks and the lilypad sank
The whole project a failure

What does the naked man say. Hot and cold, wet and dry,
 rough and
Smooth. Things are variously colored but that seems an
 impertinent
Fact. The wind is warm and dry. Lots of my skin
Is still wet.

The shadow of the naked man says, "You are too fat,
 even if you
Stand with both hands on top of your head." The shadow of a
Young man with a round head and big ears; it doesn't know
How old it is.

In order to be calm and mellow
One must take time to find out what it is and practice it
So that when the atmosphere becomes busy and buggy,
 everybody
Rushing about, seeking who to blame for the confusion
They are so industriously creating . . . .
Calm mellowness may not be necessary to me
But will be there for other folks to enjoy—supposing anybody
In all the world is interested in these commodities.
The noisy creek reminds me of silk weaving looms in Kyoto.

Tassajara
6-7:III:79

And Then...

Everything else begins or stops
Talking into sleepy ears of night
Coals far down are bright red universe of another size
Only a few square inches but still hot as ever, all connected
All perfectly understandable, all night. Go home by moonlight.
Beyond that the molecules divide it up among themselves.
Whether we walk or stand still, very tiny threads provide us
With news of moonlight or we are paralyzed and forget
The multiplication table.

When they are awake they don't remember having listened all
night.
Do you follow my drift (I think all that part is about
A gold mine)
A veritable treasure underground
Out to lunch, off the wall, down the tubes
The sun is in Chicago.

Tassajara
29 or 30:IV:79

The Ghosts

Of people dead fifty years and not only people—
Theaters and streetcars and large hotels follow me
Into this dusty little gully. None of them ever liked California
Why don't they stay in Portland where they belong.
I'm tired of them.

A new ghost in this morning's dream,
Beautiful and young and still alive
How far will that one follow me? I'm not chasing any,
Any more.

Tassajara
14:VII:79

The Phantom of Delight

The candy glass taking shape and color
Of brown soup to remind us
That part is all we know about the whole thing
And IS the whole thing
The "beauty" or aesthetic shock
Points at that or nothing

The glass mug shines
Brown and colorless
Exquisite; complete.

Tassajara
10:VIII:79

Divine Poisons

Do something else. Change everything
Today begins the new life. Today went away.
Change continues.   Radioactive Materials.

What does anybody know about Hawaii?

*

It's all
PSYCHOLOGICAL 

*

The corners of this room open out
Into infinite space if I look into them
Crosseyed.

*

watch it!

Tassajara
23 or 24:VIII:79

Labor Day Again, 1979 at San Francisco

News and music all day long.
The great black cat is fatter and older, just like me.
Firecrackers.
Breaking bottles, windows, cars, brains, airplanes
All crumbling back into original plywood, cardboard, baling
  wire
Threats, menaces, tears and recriminations:

The President rides a steam calliope
Up and down the Mississippi River
"Keeping in touch" with everybody through music, television,
Steam power

A young person fluttering on the streetcorner told me,
"You're so false!", teetering on a pair of high wooden *cothurni*
"Don't fall down," I replied, as it wavered down Laguna St
Repeating, "You're so false!"

San Francisco
3:IX:79

HOT SPRINGS INFERNAL IN THE HUMAN BEAST

Examine a big stone across the creek outside the kitchen
window
Instead of walking out to coffee? Saved by the real world
again!
Walk.
Get away from here? Go read thermometer in the garden;
Fingernails unaccountably dirty.

hummingbird

I gross and unwieldy, torpid and silent
I must begin to flap new plumes, great wings
And sing a one-eyed song of Halicarnassus in the spring
Old and immense and hastening to die
Clutch wildly at any spark of life

hummingbird

Yellow anemone
Purple morning Glory
Four nasturtiums (O R A N G E)

Tassajara
5:X:79

Homage to Hart Crane

As golden yellow as possible
The rocks blue-green as T'ang Dynasty
Clothing colors mudded out–red, yellow, blue, green, black
Animals, imaginary lions, elephants and tigers
Realistic birds. I need a big collection of Crayolas.

Image flowers in mirror landscape sexier
Under glass, poem or picture
Reflection statuary reflecting lights and images
Are there many places.
Only by looking at small details of moss or flower centers
Through a magnifying glass

"uncathected Oedipal backlash; schizoid mirror worlds
of brilliant silence"

Now I find I've skipped all carelessly onto this page
Leaving the opening preceding this one blank
Fetch the colors! Summon the genius!

Restriction of the view by round window frame
Lends something of the thick
Unobtainable silence of mirrors
When looking at a distant landscape from a great height
Something of the same feeling occurs
The part of the world "over there," mountains &c
Is absolutely silent
While the place where one stands is nearly still.
Hell yes.
A distinct blue line. The thread of the discourse
Tightens up too much; puckers the fabric.

Tassajara
23-26:X:79

What Are You Studying, These Days?

The electronic watch runs backwards to five A.M.
At night I read with broken eyes
How to control the Universe: compel with mantra, mandala,
  vision—
Summon, seal, dissolve, bind, subjugate & destroy &c
Powers to do what is already being done anyway
"Power to do good," or "Sufficient unto the day is the evil
  thereof"
"Sweet Analytics, 'tis thou hast ravish'd me"

The Merry-go-round, the Ferris wheel
The shoot-the-chutes

Your trouble is you're not very real, are you.
Hallucinatory fountain pens, eh?
Skin chips and flaky on the outside
Internal organs all blackened and shriveled
What do you expect with too much in mind
Too busy to see or hear a single particular?
I have put on a gown of power I didn't know I had—
Or wanted.

Tassajara
20:XI:79

Songs

1.

Eat a little now
Eat a little later
Eat a little alligator
        Now

2.

Sing Galveston
Sing Amarillo
Your Daddy was
An armadillo

Sing Coeur d'Alene
Sing Pocatello
Your Mother played
A mouldy Cello

3.

You pleaded
                on your bended knee
You spoke as handsome
                as could be
You was wearing your
                very best Brooks Brothers Suit
When you biodegraded me

I really believed
                everything you said
I probably wasn't quite
                right in the head

Now you've left
                    town and I
                    wish I was dead
'Cause you biodegraded me, &c. &c.

Chanson d'Outre Tombe

They said we was nowhere
Actually we are beautifully embalmed
      in Pennsylvania
They said we wanted too much.
Gave too little, a swift hand-job
            no vaseline.
We were geniuses with all kinds
      embarrassing limitations
O if only we would realize our potential
O if only that awful self-indulgence
& that shoddy politics of irresponsibility
O if only we would grow up, shut up, die
& so we did & do & chant beyond
      the cut-rate grave digged by
            indignant reviewers
O if we would only lay down & stay
      THERE—In California, Pennsylvania
Whence we keep leaking out nasty radioactive
    waste like old plutonium factory
Wrecking your white expensive world

Tassajara
27 III 1979

Wherever trees and mountain rivers
fishy oceans
Ah!
flowery caves
feathery crystals
There yes a-living eye shine
O
Man and
Woman
Sings color shape whenever
Moon fire words together
Go
Take
Summon

29:IV:78

MAYFLY

KEEP HITTING ON
PALO ALTO
O PRAGMATIST
HEURISTICALLY
BECAUSE I WANT
SOMETHING
{NO OTHER CAUSE}

I SUFFER I SAY I HURT,
KNOWLEDGABLY – TO
LIVE WITH ALL.

29 : IV : 78

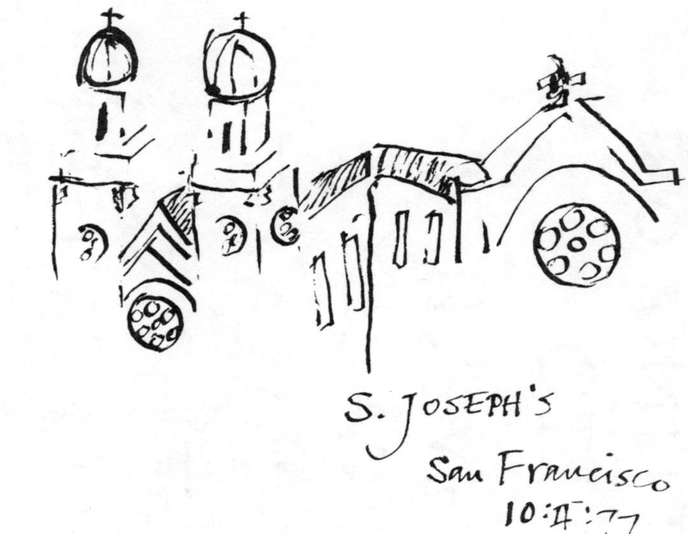

S. JOSEPH'S

San Francisco

10:II:77

big & old & expensive
the two little towers
actual GOLDEN tips
for emphasis.
a cock-eyed crocket
crossed

Philip Whalen

19/20 : IV : 73
Philip Whalen

One color only

Wm Cowper
Mary Unwin

Have you
thought
of using RED
ink
?

Olney,
{Bucks.}
ENGLAND

"why don't you write a novel
& make some money?" jack asked.
{Berkeley, Calif.}

"_Non_ _Angli_ _sed_ _angeli_," the Pope said; "There's
no such thing as a bad boy."

and then it
was that there
appeared

le chat énorme

ce chat ci-
immonde

incontestable,
&c.

15 XI 78
Philip Whalen

Why should you listen
Because you can't hear what's written down
You need straight poop more than anything else
Now I've talked too long
None of this reaches you at all.

20 III : 73

Philip Whalen

{ I never learned to like
South America. }

{ Marigold petals
are square at the end }

Comma, too long to reach
you all

a marigold
& some anemones
the japanese vase made by some
American

INDEX OF TITLES & FIRST LINES

First lines are set in italics

ACKNOWLEDGMENTS

Some of these poems have appeared in the following named magazines: *Bezoar, Bombay Gin, Brilliant Corners, Big Sky, Foot,* and *The Ark* (Minneapolis). Thanks also to Mr Lew Hartman for the loan of some typing paper on which to copy the manuscript.

The poem, "For Clark Coolidge," was produced as one of a portfolio of six holograph poems by several authors lithographed by Charles Gill in a very limited edition from the Graphic Arts Workshop at the California College of Arts and Crafts at Oakland, California.

Grey Fox Books

GUY DAVENPORT
Herakleitos and Diogenes

EDWARD DORN
Selected Poems

ALLEN GINSBERG
The Gates of Wrath: Rhymed Poems 1948–1952
Gay Sunshine Interview (with Allen Young)
Improvised on the Tongue

JACK KEROUAC
Heaven & Other Poems

MICHAEL McCLURE
Hymns to St. Geryon & Dark Brown

FRANK O'HARA
Early Writing
Poems Retrieved
Standing Still and Walking in New York

CHARLES OLSON
The Post Office

MICHAEL RUMAKER
A Day and a Night at the Baths

GARY SNYDER
He Who Hunted Birds in His Father's Village: The Dimensions of a Haida Myth
Riprap

GARY SNYDER, LEW WELCH & PHILIP WHALEN
On Bread & Poetry

JACK SPICER
One Night Stand & Other Poems

LEW WELCH
How I Work as a Poet & Other Essays / Plays / Stories
I, Leo—An Unfinished Novel
I Remain: The Letters of Lew Welch & the Correspondence of His Friends
Ring of Bone: Collected Poems 1950–1971
Selected Poems
Trip Trap (with Jack Kerouac & Albert Saijo)

PHILIP WHALEN
Decompressions: Selected Poems
Scenes of Life at the Capital
Enough Said

Cans 7
poetics 20,55
change 25